ARIANNA'S MAGIC BOOTS

By: Karen A. Gasperini

Arianna's Magic Boots by Karen A. Gasperini

Illustrations by Deanna M.

©2017 Karen A. Gasperini

This book is dedicated to my daughter Arianna Ta'Mari Robinson and all the other children like my daughter and I who are living with a disability. Arianna and I have BEALS Syndrome, severe scoliosis, anxiety, asthma, and club feet. We don't let our disabilities stop us from dreaming and pushing to reach our goals. Please follow your heart and don't let anyone or anything stop you from being who you truly are.

Author's Thank you's

To my family and friends for their love & support.

To my physical therapist Kevin Muldowney, author of *"Living Life to the Fullest with Ehlers-Danlos Syndrome: Guide to Living a Better Quality of Life While Having EDS"* for helping me get stronger each day.

To Arianna's physical therapist, Mrs. Jane Corrigan Valerio-Calamar for always being there for her. We appreciate you.

To my dear friend, Dangelo Hunt author of the children's book series *"I Wanna Be A"* for his guidance and support on this new writing journey for me.

The bright morning light woke Arianna up from a deep sleep. She sat up and stretched. Arianna knew she had to get up. She couldn't be late for therapy.

She ran into the bathroom
to brush her teeth.

After she finished her breakfast, Arianna dressed in her favorite outfit.

Next, she put on her (AFOs) leg braces and sneakers. She calls them her "magic boots" because they take her on adventures. All she has to do is stomp three times and say, "Away we go!" and the adventure begins.

On our way to physical therapy.

They met Arianna's physical therapist and her name is Mrs. Jane. She, helps Arianna do exercises to make her bones stronger and helps her build stamina and balance.

Next, Arianna held Mrs. Jane's hand and walked to the railings to start her exercises.

Arianna slowly put both hands on each railing and started to follow Mrs. Jane down the path.

As Arianna walked, she noticed a new poster of jungle animals on the wall.

She thought to herself "I wish I could go to the jungle instead of therapy today." Arianna looked down at her magic boots. Then she closed her eyes, stomped three times and said, "Away we go."

When Arianna opened
her eyes, she was in a
jungle surrounded by
animals. Her magic
boots turned into
safari boots.

The magic in Arianna's safari boots gave her bananas to help her feed the monkeys and peanuts to feed the elephants.

As Arianna waved good-bye to her new furry friends, she noticed that one of the baby monkeys had wandered away from her mama. "Can you help me find my mama?" asked the baby monkey. Arianna said, "I would be glad to help."

Arianna and the baby monkey crossed the lake to look for the baby monkey's mama, but she wasn't there.

The two new friends searched high and low.

She still was nowhere
to be found.

Finally, the two buddies came to a waterfall where the baby monkey takes her bath in every morning, and there they saw the baby monkey's mama.

The monkey family was so happy to have her back that they gave Arianna lots of bananas to say thank you.

Arianna hugged the baby monkey goodbye.

Arianna knew it was getting late so, she closed her eyes, stomped three times and said, "Away we go."

When she opened her eyes, her therapy session with Mrs. Jane was over.

Arianna's mother asked if she had fun at therapy. Arianna said, "I had a lot of fun and can't wait to go back."

Arianna and her mom
waved goodbye to
Mrs. Jane.

Back at home, time to wash up for lunch.

Time for lunch...

Arianna's mother asked, "Where are your leg braces and sneakers?" Arianna smiled and said "They're taking a nap."

Author's Notes

"Arianna's Magic Boots," is based on Karen's daughter Arianna and herself. Growing up Karen and her daughter wore leg braces to help with their clubfeet. One of their favorite things to do when wearing their leg braces (AFOs) was using their imagination to go on adventures. Karen resides in Rhode Island with her family.

Arianna Age 5 with her little friend Pearl (2007)

Karen and her leg braces with her little brother Isaiah by her side. (1988)

Made in the USA
Middletown, DE
10 March 2019